Welcome

IT'S THE GREATEST football tournament on the planet. It's the competition every player and every fan hopes their team will win. Every four years supporters around the globe will watch in amazement as the events of the World Cup unfold.

There will be surprise results as teams battle to make it past the group stages. At least one side regarded as an underdog will pull off a shock result or two as a big name side fails to live up to its top-billing. New stars will be born. Wonder goals will be scored. Some superstars will fail to live up to the expectations of the fans but other players will make a name for themselves and earn big money transfers to leading leagues.

There isn't anything like the World Cup. There's no big-money prize to be earned for lifting what is one of the smallest trophies in the game. But winning the most-treasured piece of silverware in football is a dream every professional and supporter would love to experience – the teams and players over the following pages have been lucky enough to live that dream...

Colin Mitchell, Editor

www.shoot.co.uk

£6.99

1930

VENUE: Uruguay
WINNERS: Uruguay
TEAMS COMPETING: 13
UK AND IRELAND: None took part as they had withdrawn from FIFA, world football's governing body.

IT TOOK LESS than a year to organise the first World Cup finals with Olympic champions Uruguay handed the job of host nation.

Nine of the sides who took part were from South America although a number of European sides declined to take part because they would have had to sail to the finals, a journey that took a number of weeks!

Semi-finals
Argentina 6 USA 1
Uruguay 6 Yugoslavia 1

Final
Uruguay 4 Argentina 2
In front of 90,000 mostly home fans Uruguay took the lead but Argentina struck back twice before half-time. The hosts scored twice more in the second 45 minutes to win the final in Montevideo, contested by the best teams in the event.

Never to be forgotten moment...
France's **Lucien Laurent** earned his place in history as scorer of the first-ever goal at the finals as his country won their open fixture against Mexico 4-1.

1934

VENUE: Italy
WINNERS: Italy
TEAMS COMPETING: 32
UK AND IRELAND: All again absent from the finals.

HOLDERS URUGUAY declined to defend their title. The 32 teams who entered had to qualify for the finals and 12 of the 16 who got through were European sides.

Semi-finals
Italy 1 Austria 0
Czechoslovakia 3 Germany 1

Final
Italy 2 Czechoslovakia 1 aet

The hosts were stunned when a long-range effort from Puc put the Czechs in front following a corner in the 70th minute. But the 45,000 crowd in Rome saw Raimondo Orsi equalise eight minutes from the end to force extra-time. Angelo Schiavio hit the winner as Italy bounced back to form in the latter stages of the game.

Never to be forgotten moment...
Spain and **Italy** drew 2-2 after extra-time and played again the following day to decide who would make the semi-finals. Italy edged the second game 1-0.

1938

VENUE: France **WINNERS:** Italy
TEAMS COMPETING: 36
UK AND IRELAND: Still no sign of England, Scotland, Wales or Northern Ireland, although the Republic of Ireland entered but failed to qualify.

HOLDERS ITALY and hosts France were given automatic qualification to the finals, a tradition still in place today. Incredibly, Brazil were the only South American side to take part.

Semi-finals
Italy 2 Brazil 1
Hungary 5 Sweden 1

Final
Italy 4 Hungary 2

Italy became the first side to retain the World Cup after dominating the final against Hungary in Paris. Colaussi and Piola got two goals each. Titkos and Sarosi scored for the runners-up in front of 45,000 fans.

Never to be forgotten moment...
This was the last tournament before World War II and Italy's Sports Minister removed the cup from his government's 'safe-keeping' and it was hidden in a shoebox under a bed!

1950

VENUE: Brazil
WINNERS: Uruguay
TEAMS COMPETING: 32
UK AND IRELAND: England, Northern Ireland, Scotland and Wales entered. Republic of Ireland also there.

ENGLAND AND SCOTLAND qualified for the finals but the Tartan Army turned down their place! India also refused to play because they weren't allowed to turn out in bare feet! Qualifiers were played in four groups, taking in Europe and the near east; South America; North and Central America; and Asia.

Finals

The format of the tournament changed with four teams, Uruguay, Brazil, Sweden and Spain competing in a final league of three matches each.

After a 7-1 win against Sweden and a 6-1 victory over Spain, Brazil were favourites to win. A draw against Uruguay - who had beaten Sweden and drawn with Spain - would have been enough. But in Rio de Janeiro the Brazilians went down 2-1.

Never to be forgotten moment...

England's team – humbled 1-0 by the USA – included future Three Lions boss **Sir Alf Ramsey** and legendary players **Billy Wright, Tom Finney, Stan Mortensen** and **Wilf Mannion**.

1954

VENUE: Switzerland
WINNERS: Germany
TEAMS COMPETING: 38
UK AND IRELAND: All four home nations, plus the Republic of Ireland, entered. Only England and Scotland qualified.

THE TOURNAMENT went back to its traditional format of 16 qualifying teams who would then go through group stages to semi-finals and the final. England went out at the quarter-final stage, beaten 4-2 by Uruguay. Scotland exited at the group stage their two games resulting in a 1-0 defeat to Austria and the 7-1 hammering at the hands of Uruguay.

Semi-finals
Germany 6 Austria 1
Hungary 2 Uruguay 2 (aet)

Final
Germany 3 Hungary 2
The legendary Ferenc Puskas was recalled by Hungary for the final and obliged with a goal as his side raced into a 2-0 lead within eight minutes. A further eight minutes into the game and it was level at 2-2. Germany went into the lead despite being the relative underdogs and survived a 'goal' ruled offside in the last few minutes.

Never to be forgotten moment...
Most of the matches were played in and around the city of Berne – and for the first time fans were able to watch games on television thanks to the arrival of black and white footage to their homes.

Switzerland 1954

1958

VENUE: Sweden
WINNERS: Brazil
TEAMS COMPETING: 55
UK AND IRELAND: All competed.

ENGLAND, NORTHERN IRELAND and Scotland all reached the last 16. The Republic of Ireland lost out to England in the qualifiers. In the race to the quarter-finals, England lost 1-0 to Russia, Northern Ireland beat Czechoslovakia 2-1, Wales defeated Hungary 2-1. Scotland finished bottom of their group and were already on the way home. France saw off Northern Ireland 4-0 in the quarters and brave Wales lost by the only goal of the game to Brazil.

Semi-finals
Sweden 3 West Germany 1
Brazil 5 France 2

Final
Brazil 5 Sweden 2
The hosts took the lead in a rain-drenched Stockholm but the South Americans were 2-1 up by half-time and made it 4-1 after the interval. Sweden got a second to give themselves hope before a young Pele got his second of the game to seal victory.

Never to be forgotten moment...
The stunning arrival of **Pele** at the age of 17. He hit the winner against Wales, a hat-trick against France in the semis and grabbed two more goals in the final. But Frenchman **Juste Fontaine** set a record for the finals with 13 goals.

Sweden 1958

Chile 1962

1962

VENUE: Chile
WINNERS: Brazil
TEAMS COMPETING: 56
UK AND IRELAND: All four home nations, plus the Republic of Ireland, took part. But only England managed to get past the qualifying stages to reach the actual finals.

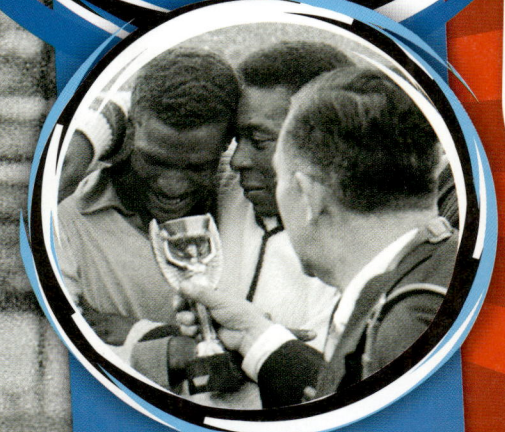

Semi-finals
Brazil 4 Chile 2
Czechoslovakia 3 Yugoslavia 1

Final
Brazil 3 Czechoslovakia 1

Brazil lost the influential Pele when he picked up a foot injury in their second game of the tournament, ironically against the Czechs who they faced in the final. It didn't look good when the Europeans took the lead in Santiago but before half-time Brazil were level and early in the second 45 minutes were ahead. A terrible mistake by their keeper ensured the final scoreline and saw Brazil retain the trophy.

ENGLAND QUALIFIED for the finals from their three-team group which included Portugal and Luxembourg. Northern Ireland and Wales bombed out at the qualifying stages. The Republic of Ireland finished bottom of their qualifiers with four defeats, whilst Scotland and the Czechs tied in the same group, the Tartan Army losing a play-off. England were second in the first round group at the finals, behind Hungary and ahead of Argentina and Bulgaria, but the Three Lions bowed out 3-1 in the quarter-finals to Brazil. The Brazilians had gone into to the finals with nine members of the team who had won four years earlier.

Never to be forgotten moment...

Brazil's **Garrincha** was hit on the head by a bottle thrown by a fan and police had to drag Italy's **Ferrini** off the pitch after he had been red-carded in an all-out war of a game with Chile. Another Italian, **David**, also got his marching orders as fists flew and tempers flared.

England's finest hour

1966

VENUE: England
WINNERS: England
TEAMS COMPETING: 71
UK AND IRELAND: England qualified as hosts. Northern Ireland failed by one point to qualify. Wales and Scotland were second in their groups. The Republic of Ireland failed to beat Spain in a play-off after the sides won a game each in a two team qualifying group!

MANAGER ALF RAMSEY had been ridiculed and mocked for almost three years after he predicted that his England side would win the World Cup on home soil.

THE FORMER ENGLAND full-back and ex-Ipswich boss was the victim of even more hatred when he overlooked fans' favourite Jimmy Greaves to leave Geoff Hurst in his side for the final.

But at the end of an epic 90 minutes followed by a pulsating period of extra-time the chant of 'Ramsey, Ramsey, Ramsey' echoed around the historic Wembley Stadium.

The serious-faced boss refused to take any of the credit away from the squad he had backed to the hilt and stood on the sidelines as they milked the praise of the 93,800 supporters in the ground.

When skipper Bobby Moore lifted the trophy to prove the Three Lions ruled the world Ramsey went to kiss the World Cup but refused to lay his hands on the silverware.

How the teams progressed

Group 1 — Wembley and White City Stadium

	P	W	D	L	F	A	P
England	3	2	1	0	4	0	5
Uruguay	3	1	2	0	2	1	4
Mexico	3	0	2	1	1	3	2
France	3	0	1	2	2	5	1

England kicked off the finals with a drab goal-less draw against Uruguay. Five days later they got the expected victory over Mexico with a 2-0 scoreline and four days after that had an unconvincing 2-0 win over France.

Group 2 — Hillsborough and Villa Park

	P	W	D	L	F	A	P
W. Germany	3	2	1	0	7	1	5
Argentina	3	2	1	0	4	1	5
Spain	3	1	0	2	4	5	2
Switzerland	3	0	0	3	1	9	0

Germany got off to a flying start with a 5-0 hammering of Switzerland at Sheffield Wednesday's Hillsborough but were held to a 0-0 at Villa Park by Argentina. Aston Villa's ground was where they completed the group with a 2-1 win over Spain.

Group 3 — Goodison Park and Old Trafford

	P	W	D	L	F	A	P
Portugal	3	3	0	0	9	2	6
Hungary	3	2	0	1	7	5	4
Brazil	3	1	0	2	4	6	2
Bulgaria	3	0	0	3	1	8	0

Portugal began with a 3-1 win at Old Trafford against Hungary and then a 3-0 victory over Bulgaria at Man United's ground. They had another 3-1 win in their final fixture at Goodison Park – over reigning champions Brazil!

Group 4 — Ayresome Park (Middlesbrough) and Roker Park (Sunderland)

	P	W	D	L	F	A	P
USSR	3	3	0	0	6	1	6
N.Korea	3	1	1	1	2	4	3
Italy	3	1	0	2	2	2	2
Chile	3	0	1	2	2	5	1

USSR kicked off at Ayresome Park by trouncing North Korea 3-0, got a 1-0 victory over Italy at Roker and were again on Wearside for their 2-1 win against Chile.

Quarter-finals

England 1 Argentina 0

England were still unconvincing in a tough match at Wembley against ten-man Argentina. It was **Geoff Hurst**, in the side for the injured **Jimmy Greaves**, who finally broke the deadlock in the 77th minute with a header over the keeper.

W. Germany 4 Uruguay 0

A goal down after the ball was deflected into the net at Hillsborough, Uruguay had a penalty appeal turned down and then lost the plot. With two men sent off they conceded three more goals in the second-half.

Portugal 5 N. Korea 3

The North Koreans were the surprise package of the finals and showed their skill, determination and courage by taking a three-goal lead at Goodison Park against Portugal. But the great **Eusebio** hit two goals before half-time and two more after the break with Augusto chipping in in the fifth.

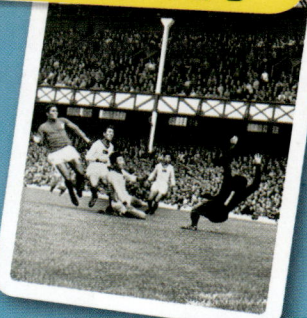

USSR 2 Hungary 1

Hungary played well at Roker Park but two goalkeeping mistakes saw them go 2-0 down before they grabbed a late consolation.

Semi-finals

W. Germany 2 USSR 1

The in-form Germans were expected to conquer the USSR at Goodison Park. The Russian were already a goal down when they had a player red-carded. Two goals behind until the dying seconds they pulled one back right at the death.

England 2 Portugal 1

England finally showed some form in an exciting game at Wembley where they defended well and turned on the attacking class. **Bobby Charlton** scored both goals and saw his side concede a penalty.

Third place

Portugal 2 USSR 1

Eusebio scored his fourth penalty in three games before the USSR equalised through **Malofeyev**. **Torres** hit the winner late on.

Final

England 4 W. Germany 2

Germany took the lead after just 12 minutes through Helmut Haller. But seven minutes later Geoff Hurst had the teams level.

Thirteen minutes from time Hurst deflect a shot to Martin Peters who scored spectacularly and England were 2-1 ahead.

With just a minute to go England's otherwise resolute defence conceded a free-kick which produced a loose ball in the penalty area and Wolfgang Webber stuck it into the back of the net to send the match into extra-time.

This period of play produced three of the most memorable moments of a World Cup Final.

First was the decision by a Russian linesman 11 minutes into extra-time to confirm that Hurst's effort had hit the crossbar, bounced on the ground and crossed the line to give England a 3-2 lead. This incident is still debated.

Second, Hurst scored again just a minute from time to make it 4-2 and become the only scorer of a hat-trick in a World Cup Final.

Third, as Hurst's third goal went into the net, BBC TV commentator Kenneth Wolstenholme uttered the words that no football fan will ever forget: "Some people are on the pitch, they think it's all over… it is now!"

Never to be forgotten moment…

Geoff Hurst's was it over the line or wasn't it 'goal' – who needs goal line technology?

Golden guys throw in the towels!

They may have taken part in English football's most famous victory but the 22 players called up for the 1966 World Cup Finals had to face some harsh realities.

Forget massive match fees, first class accommodation, luxury transport and every desire and whim catered for like today's megastars have come to expect.

Those who took part in games got a £60 match fee, reserves received £30 and trainers £30.

The Football Association provided them with shirts, shorts and stockings – but the players were expected to take along their own towels, gym shoes, shinguards, spikes and two pairs of football boots.

They also had to have a suit in which to travel and another for evening wear!

The players were also banned from talking to newspapers, TV and radio after games.

World Cup programme

Beer, spirts and cigarette advertising dominated the official World Cup Final programme which cost two shillings and six pence (12.5p).

The covers were in colour but the rest of the glossy publication was in black and white looking nothing like the glitzy programmes fans have come to expect today

England's heroes — The 11 winners!

- **Geoff Hurst** (West Ham)
- **Roger Hunt** (Liverpool)
- **Martin Peters** (West Ham)
- **Nobby Stiles** (Man United)
- **Alan Ball** (Blackpool)
- **Bobby Charlton** (Man United)
- **Jack Charlton** (Leeds)
- **Bobby Moore** (West Ham)
- **George Cohen** (Fulham)
- **Ray Wilson** (Everton)
- **Gordon Banks** (Leicester City)

...and the rest of the squad

Jimmy Greaves (Tottenham); John Connelly (Man United); Ron Springett (Sheffield Wednesday); Peter Bonetti (Chelsea); Jimmy Armfield (Blackpool); Gerry Byrne (Liverpool); Ron Flowers (Wolves); Norman Hunter (Leeds); Terry Paine (Southampton); Ian Callaghan (Liverpool); George Eastham (Arsenal).

Mexico 1970

1970

VENUE: Mexico
WINNERS: Brazil
TEAMS COMPETING: 70
UK AND IRELAND: All took part, England qualified as holders. Once again they were the only home nation to play past the qualifying stages. The Republic of Ireland also failed to board a plane to Mexico.

Semi-finals
Brazil 3 Uruguay 1
Italy 4 West Germany 3 (aet)

Final
Brazil 4 Italy 1

Brazil were the favourites and backed by the Azteca Stadium crowd they got off to a flyer with a simple header from Pele. But Boninsegna grabbed an equaliser and it was game on!
The relentless Brazilians finally wore down the Italians' resolute defence with strikes from Gerson and then Jairzinho.
But it was the later stages of the game that saw Brazil snatch possession and put together a seven-player move that resulted in Carlos Alberto stroking the ball into the net.

WITH THE THREE LIONS guaranteed a place at the finals to defend their title, Wales, Northern Ireland Scotland and the Republic of Ireland faced the qualifiers. Wales lost all four of their qualifying games. Northern Ireland finished second in a three-team group, pipped for a qualifying place by the USSR (Russia). Scotland couldn't get past the might of West Germany although they did finish ahead of Austria and Cyprus. The Republic of Ireland took just one point and finished bottom of a group that was won by Hungary and included Denmark and Czechoslovakia. England beat Romania 1-0 in their opening group game and Czechoslovakia by a single penalty in their third. In between they suffered defeat by the same score against Brazil.
The blistering heat and high altitude had put England at a big disadvantage but they battled bravely before being destroyed by a moment of genius by Pele. England had done enough to finish second in the group and reach the quarter-finals. Here they took a two-goal lead against Germany before being pegged back to 2-2, forcing the game into extra time. The best team lost as the Germans went through with a late goal, stand-in keeper Peter Bonetti being criticised for his performance.

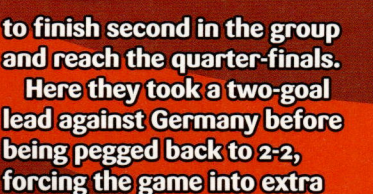

Never to be forgotten moment...

The legendary diving save by keeper **Gordon Banks** that prevented an almost certain goal from a brilliant header by **Pele**. Pictures show skipper **Bobby Moore** already in despair as he believed the shot was in the net.

West Germany 1974

1974

VENUE: West Germany
WINNERS: West Germany
TEAMS COMPETING: 99
UK AND IRELAND: Only Scotland reached the final 16 for the finals which had a change of format for this tournament. The other home nations stumbled at the qualifying hurdle. The Republic of Ireland could count themselves unlucky not to get through.

Play-off for third and fourth

Poland 1 Brazil 0

Final

West Germany 2 Holland 1

No Germany player had touched the ball when Player of the Tournament Johan Cruyff was brought down in the area and Johan Neeskens put the silky Dutch ahead from the spot.

The steely Germans were driven on by Franz Beckenbauer and against the run of play they equalised from the penalty spot through Paul Breitner.

Gerd Muller, playing his last international, hit home from close range before half-time. It was his 14th in all finals, a new record for the tournament.

POLAND BECAME the arch enemies of England during qualifying. England beat and drew with Wales in qualifying and then lost to Poland.

A victory against the Poles in their final game would have got them through but they could only draw and, like the Welsh, didn't make the finals.

The Republic of Ireland were group runners-up to the USSR, who were later banned. Northern Ireland finished third in their group of four behind Bulgaria and Portugal.

Scotland disposed of Czechoslovakia and Denmark only to be paired with Brazil in the first group of final matches, along with Yugoslavia and Zaire.

The Tartan Army celebrated when Billy Bremner's men opened with the expected 2-0 victory over Zaire and were still happy with a goal-less draw against Brazil. Their final game was a 1-1 draw.

Three teams all had four points but Yugoslavia topped the group, Brazil were second and Scotland third, the outcome settled by goal difference.

There was next two groups of eight to produce a play-off and the finalists.

Never to be forgotten moment...

Scotland flew home unbeaten – but with their reputations intact, especially that of inspirational captain **Billy Bremner**.

Argentina 1978

1978

VENUE: Argentina
WINNERS: Argentina
TEAMS COMPETING: 106
UK AND IRELAND: England failed on goal difference to get past Italy in the qualifiers; Northern Ireland were third in a four-team group; Republic of Ireland and Wales were bottom of their groups.

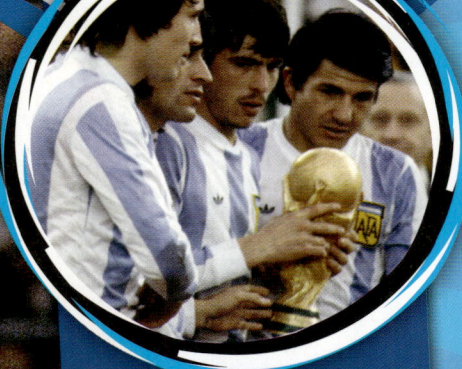

ONCE AGAIN Scotland were the only home nation to qualify for the finals having put out Czechoslovakia and Wales. The Tartan Army beat eventual finalists Holland 3-2 in the first group stage with two goals from Archie Gemmell and one from Kenny Dalglish but by then it was too late – they had already lost 3-1 to Peru and drawn 1-1 with Iran.
Holland had a slow start but by the time they had hammered Austria 5-1, drawn 2-2 with Germany and beaten Italy 2-1 in the second round of games to top their group they were looking good. Argentina had won through to the final thanks to a second round 6-0 win against Peru, 2-0 against Poland and a goal-less draw against lackluster Brazil.

Play-off for 3rd-4th
Brazil 2 Italy 1

Final
Argentina 3 Holland 1 (aet)
Gamesmanship, time-wasting and a mostly patriotic 77,000 crowd in Buenos Aries didn't help the brave Dutch against Argentina.
The Netherlands went behind after 37 minutes when Mario Kempes scored and it wasn't until the 81st minute that their battling got them level through substitute Dick Nanninga. Kempes added a second for Argentina 14 minutes into extra-time before Daniel Bertoni sealed the home victory.

Never to be forgotten moment...
Argentina were set the task of having to win their final group game by four clear goals to beat fellow South Americans **Brazil** for a place in the final. They won 6-0!

21

Spain 1982

Algeria v Austria

1982

VENUE: Spain
WINNERS: Italy
TEAMS COMPETING: 108
UK AND IRELAND: England returned to the finals after a 12-year absence despite being runners-up to Hungary in the qualifiers. Scotland and Northern Ireland went through from the same group. Wales and the Republic of Ireland fell at the first hurdle.

Semi-finals
Italy 2 Poland 0
West Germany 3 France 3
(aet, W. Germany won 5-4 on pens)

Final
Italy 3 West Germany 1

After Antonio Cabrini fired a first-half penalty wide the Italians must have been wondering if they were right out of luck.

But the Germans showed signs of tiredness after their gruelling semi-final battle and Paolo Rossi - the tournament's Golden Boot winner - headed the Italians in front after 57 minutes.

Twelve minutes later Marco Tardelli fired home a second and nine minutes from time Alessandro Altobelli made it 3-0. Paul Breitner grabbed a late consolation on 83 minutes.

FOR THE FIRST TIME 24 teams were allowed to reach the finals. England soon staked their claim for a place in the second round with wins over France, Czechoslovakia and Kuwait which gave them victory in their group.

Northern Ireland stunned the hosts with a 1-0 victory thanks to Gerry Armstrong, and then added a goal-less draw with Yugoslavia and a 1-1 with Honduras to also win their group.

A 5-2 win over New Zealand, a 2-2 draw with the USSR and a crushing 4-1 defeat at the hands of Brazil saw Scotland board the plane home.

Goal-less draws against West Germany and Spain meant England were homeward bound after the second round. They were joined by Northern Ireland who had a 2-2 with Austria and were beaten 4-1 by France.

Never to be forgotten moment...

Gerry Armstrong's hammer shot against Spain - where he would later play for Mallorca - earned him the British Player of the Tournament award. And England midfielder **Bryan Robson** scored the fastest-ever goal in the finals after just 27 seconds of the game against France - a best that stood until 2002.

Mexico 1986

1986

VENUE: Mexico
WINNERS: Argentina
TEAMS COMPETING: 120
UK AND IRELAND: England won their qualifying group; Northern Ireland were runners-up in the same group and qualified. The Republic of Ireland were fourth in qualifying. Scotland beat Australia in a play-off to advance. Wales were third in Scotland's group.

Semi-finals
West Germany 2 France 0
Argentina 2 Belgium 0

Final
Argentina 3 West Germany 2
The 114,600 fans in Mexico City's Azteca Stadium saw a classic match full of high drama, even without Maradona at his glittering best.
Defender Jose Brown headed Argentina into the lead after 23 minutes and ten minutes after the break striker Jorge Valdano made it 2-0.
With 16 minutes to go the Germans looked dead and buried but midfielder Karl-Heinz Rummenigge stabbed home. With just ten minutes to go they were level when Rudi Voller headed in from a corner.
It was of course Maradona who played a telling pass with seven minutes left on the clock. It was latched on to by midfielder Jorge Burruchaga, arguably the player of the match, who beat the keeper.

TEENAGER NORMAN
Whiteside helped Northern Ireland to a 1-1 draw with Algeria. But a 2-1 defeat at the hands of Spain and a 3-0 hammering by Brazil meant the boys in green were out at the first hurdle.

Scotland lost 1-0 to Denmark, 2-1 to Germany and were held by Uruguay to a goal-less draw. Bottom of their group they also went home.

England suffered a 1-0 defeat to Portugal, drew 0-0 with Morocco and then hammered Poland 3-0 with a Gary Lineker hat-trick. Second to Morocco they progressed to the last 16.

Two more strikes from Lineker and one from Peter Beardsley saw the Lions roar past Paraguay 3-0 and into the quarter-finals.

Never to be forgotten moment...
Gary Lineker's hat-trick against Poland helped him to the Golden Boot with six goals – but it's more likely you aren't going to forget **Maradona's** 'Hand of God' goal!

Lineker was on target again against Argentina – but two earlier goals from Maradona, one his 'Hand of God' strike where he handled the ball past keeper Peter Shilton, the other a supreme bit of skill where he went past five players and then the keeper – put England out.

Italy 1990

1990

VENUE: Italy
WINNERS: Germany
TEAMS COMPETING: 112
UK AND IRELAND: England were second in their qualifying group behind Sweden; Scotland went through behind Yugoslavia. The Republic of Ireland were runners-up to Spain in a group where Northern Ireland failed to qualify. Wales were bottom of their group.

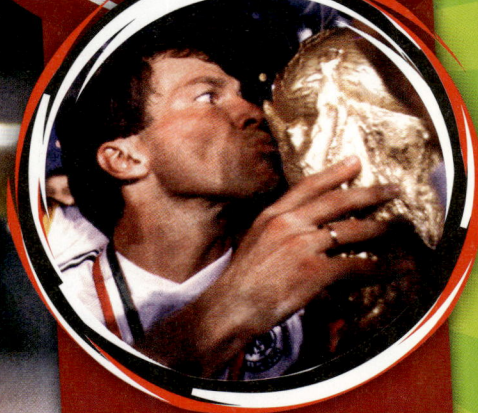

A **DISAPPOINTING** 1-0 defeat to Costa Rica and 1-0 loss to Brazil meant Scotland were soon homeward bound despite defeating Sweden 2-1 at the group stage.

England and Ireland fought out a 1-1 draw thanks to Gary Lineker and Kevin Sheedy. The Lions then had a goal-less draw with Holland and a 1-0 victory over Egypt that saw them top the group.

The Republic reached the next stage with a 0-0 against Egypt and a 1-1 with Holland that left them runners-up.

The Republic had to endure extra-time in the last 16 against Romania as both sides failed to score. Ireland won 5-4 on penalties.

England were also goal-less after 90 minutes but a David Platt strike in extra time also saw them progress to the quarter-finals.

In Rome, against the hosts, Ireland battled hard but lost out to the only goal of the game from Toto Schillaci. Bobby Robson's England team also found it tough going against a battling Cameroon side and had to play extra time with the score 2-2 after 90 minutes. David Platt had already scored in normal time, along with a Lineker spot-kick. Lineker was brought down in the box and smashed home his second penalty for a 3-2 victory.

Arguably the best match of the tournament - but a scoreline England fans will want to forget - was the clash with Germany in the semis. An Andreas Brehme free-kick that hit the bar and somehow bounced into the net gave the Germans the lead.

Ten minutes from time it was the prolific Lineker who cracked home an equaliser to force extra time. England lost the penalty shoot-out with Stuart Pearce and Chris Waddle enduring the heartbreak of missing their kicks.

Semi-finals
England 1 West Germany 1
(Germany won penalty shoot-out 4-3)
Argentina 1 Italy 1
(Argentina won penalty shoot-out 4-3)

Final
West Germany 1 Argentina 0
A boring tournament ended with a dull final! Argentina, surprisingly beaten 1-0 by Cameroon in the opening game, became the first side not to score in the final.

Even the 85th minute winner by Andreas Brehme came from the penalty spot to give the Germans their third title.

But the 90 minutes were not without incident. In the 65th minute, Argentina's Pedro Monzon became the first player sent off during a World Cup Final, following a foul on Jurgen Klinsmann.

With just four minutes to go team-mate Gustavo Dezotti also saw red for pulling down Jürgen Kohler.

Never to be forgotten moment...
Paul Gascoigne's tears when he realised his semi-final booking meant he would miss the final if England qualified - he could have kept his eyes dry!

USA 1994

1994

VENUE: USA
WINNERS: Brazil
TEAMS COMPETING: 143
UK AND IRELAND: England failed to qualify, finishing third behind Norway and Holland. Scotland and Wales were fourth in their qualifying groups. Northern Ireland were fourth in the Republic of Ireland's group – the Republic through, beaten only by Spain.

Semi-finals
Brazil 1 Sweden 0
Italy 2 Bulgaria 1

Final
Brazil 0 Italy 0
(Brazil won 3-2 on penalties)
The 94,000 fans in the Passadena Rose Bowl in Los Angeles and the one billion television viewers watching around the world witnessed the first World Cup Final decided on penalties.
A poor match went to extra-time and then the penalty shoot-out.
Marcio Santos had missed for Brazil and Franco Baresi for Italy. Romario, Branco and Dunga had all converted for Brazil, along with Albertini and Evani for the Italians.
But Daniele Massaro's miss meant that if Roberto Baggio failed from the spot Brazil would become the first team to win the cup four-times. The legendary striker, who had hit two in the semi-final, shot into the crowd...

THE REPUBLIC of Ireland became everyone's second-favourite team at the finals as Jack Charlton's men battled against the best. Their campaign got off to an incredible start in New York with a 1-0 victory over Italy thanks to Ray Houghton chesting down and smacking home after just 12 minutes.
In the sweltering heat of Florida, Garcia put Mexico two up before the men in green hit back with a John Aldridge header.
All four teams in Ireland's group finished with four points – Mexico and the Republic going through with Italy. The heroics ended in the second round when the Irish were beaten 2-0 in Orlando by a talented Holland side.

Never to be forgotten moment...
Colombian **Andres Escobar** was murdered when he returned home after giving away an own-goal against the hosts!

29

France 1998

1998

VENUE: France
WINNERS: France
TEAMS COMPETING: 178
UK AND IRELAND: England topped their qualifying group ahead of Italy. Scotland were runners-up to Austria but qualified. Wales only finished ahead of San Marino; Northern Ireland only beat Albania. The Republic of Ireland lost a play-off qualifier against Belgium.

Semi-finals
Brazil 1 Holland 1
(aet, Brazil won 4-2 on penalties)
France 2 Croatia 1

Final
France 3 Brazil 0

Ronaldo was missing from the team sheet when Brazil named their side - but 15 minutes later the striker was back in the starting line up, leaving the 80,000 fans in Paris's Stade de France totally puzzled.

France looked the better team for most of the match and took the lead with a Zinedine Zidane header after 27 minutes. He put another in with his head just before half time.

The home team looked as though they may have problems when Marcel Desailly was sent off with 20 minutes to go but Manu Petit's left-foot screamer during time added on put paid to South American hopes.

THERE WERE MANY dramatic moments in the games up to the final, including the first-ever golden goal in the knockout stages of the competition. Scotland were first in the queue at the airport for a return home after they were left stranded at the bottom of their group with just one point. They drew with Norway and were beaten by Brazil and Morocco.

England squeezed through the opening stages with 2-0 wins against Tunisia and Columbia but finished behind Romania who beat them 2-1.

The round of 16 saw England face Argentina. Michael Owen, then just 18 and a bright new hope for the Three Lions, stunned their arch-rivals with the wonder goal that really set the stage for his future appearances in white.

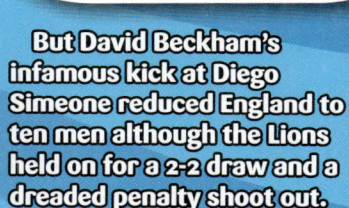

But David Beckham's infamous kick at Diego Simeone reduced England to ten men although the Lions held on for a 2-2 draw and a dreaded penalty shoot out.

Few players appeared keen to take pens and after Paul Ince missed it meant David Batty had to score. He failed and Glenn Hoddle's men were on the way home, having lost 4-3.

Never to be forgotten moment...

Take your pick! **Beckham** off, **Owen** wonder goal, **Batty** penalty miss or the mystery of what happened to **Ronaldo** before the final!

31

Japan & South Korea 2002

2002

VENUE: Japan/South Korea
WINNERS: Brazil
TEAMS COMPETING: 198
UK AND IRELAND: England won their qualifying group ahead of Germany. Northern Ireland and Wales were both fifth in their six-team groups. Scotland were one-place off qualifying. The Republic of Ireland were second in their group and won a play-off with Iran.

Semi-finals
Germany 1 South Korea 0
Brazil 1 Turkey 0

Final
Brazil 2 Germany 0

Four years earlier Ronaldo had been mysteriously off and then on the team sheet for the final and then failed to shine.

He made no mistake this time in front of 69,000 fans in Yokohama's International Stadium with two goals in the space of ten second-half minutes.

German keeper Oliver Kahn failed to hold a shot from Rivaldo after 67 minutes and Ronaldo was onto it in a flash. Ten minutes later Rivaldo stepped over the ball to give Ronaldo the easy option of side footing home his second and earn Brazil their fifth world crown.

THE MOST AMAZING moment for England fans was the side's incredible 5-1 victory in Germany during qualification when Michael Owen hit a hat-trick.

It wasn't so easy in the group stage at the finals where they drew 1-1 with Sweden and had a goal-less clash with Nigeria. The icing on the cake was a 1-0 win against Argentina thanks to a David Beckham penalty after Owen had been brought down. That meant second in the 'Group of Death' behind Sweden, same points, less goals scored.

Ireland drew 1-1 with both Cameroon and Germany and then beat Saudi Arabia 3-0. Second in their group also meant they too were through to the last 16.

Owen, Emile Heskey and an own goal helped England cruise past Denmark 3-0 and into the quarter-finals.

Ireland held Spain to 1-1 but then lost 3-2 in the penalty shoot-out after extra time.

Owen struck again in the quarter-finals to give England an unlikely lead against Brazil. But Rivaldo equalised virtually on half time. Early in the second half a wicked long-range Ronaldinho free-kick gave the South Americans the lead. The same player got a red card but even with ten men they held on.

Never to be forgotten moment...

Republic of Ireland skipper **Roy Keane** was sent home in disgrace before a ball was kicked in anger - following a very public slanging match with boss **Mick McCarthy**.

33

Germany 2006

Brazil v Australia. Tim Cahill in action.

2006

VENUE: Germany
WINNERS: Italy
TEAMS COMPETING: 194
UK AND IRELAND: England won their qualifying group of six ahead of fellow qualifiers Poland – Northern Ireland in fourth and Wales fifth. Scotland were one away from a play-off chance with third in group. The Republic of Ireland were fourth.

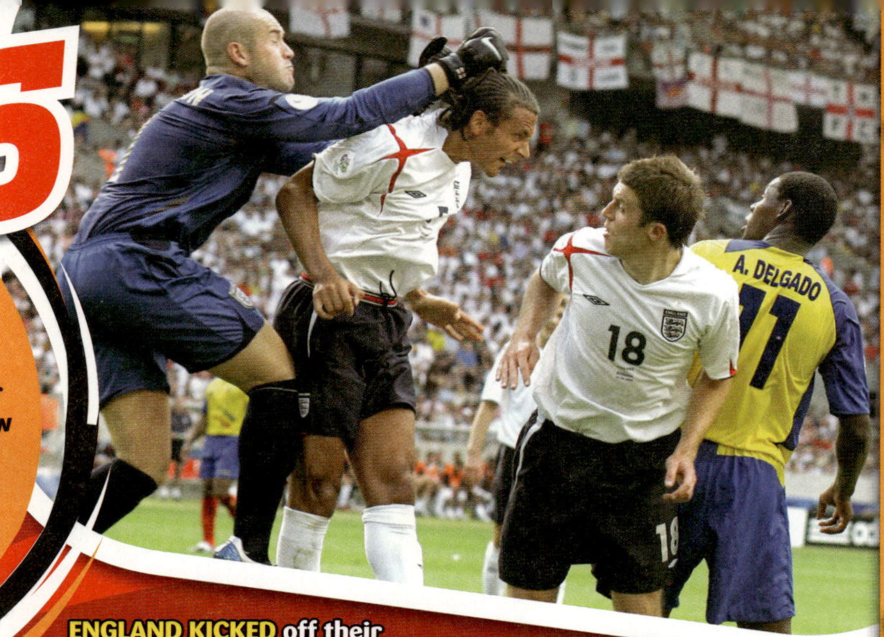

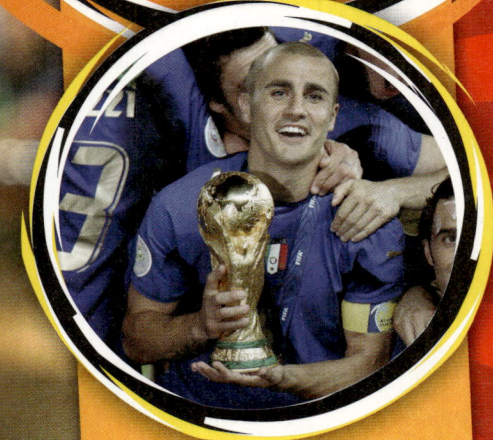

Semi-finals
Italy 2 Germany 0 (aet)
France 1 Portugal 0

Final
Italy 1 France 1
(aet, Italy won 5-3 on pens)
Zinedine Zidane was both hero and villain. He put France ahead from the penalty spot after just seven minutes but ten minutes before the end of extra-time he was red-carded.
Marco Materazzi, involved in the incident which saw Zidane sent-off, had already equalised with a header just 12 minutes after the French goal.
Ten-man France held on for the draw and during extra-time only to lose the penalty shoot-out.
The 69,000 crowd in Berlin saw Andrea Pirlo, Materazzi, Daniele de Rossi, Alessandro del Piero and Fabio Grosso score for Italy; Sylvain Wiltord, Eric Abidal and Willy Sagnol struck for France but substitute David Trezeguet missed.

ENGLAND KICKED off their group games with a lack lustre 1-0 victory against Paraguay thanks to a David Beckham free-kick that was deflected for an own-goal.
Trinidad and Tobago held out for 83 minutes before Peter Crouch and Steven Gerrard made it 2-0. A 2-2 draw with Sweden thanks to Joe Cole and Steven Gerrard ensured that Sven Goran Eriksson's Three Lions moved into the last 16.
A David Beckham strike on the hour made it 1-0 against Ecuador and put England into the quarter-finals against Portugal.
Goal-less after extra-time England again faced the dreaded penalty shoot out that had so often been their downfall – and so it was yet again. They battled bravely after Wayne Rooney was sent off after an hour for stamping on Ricardo Carvalho.
Owen Hargreaves scored from the spot but there were failures by Frank Lampard, Steven Gerrard and Jamie Carragher. Portugal scored through Simao, Helder Postiga and Cristiano Ronaldo.

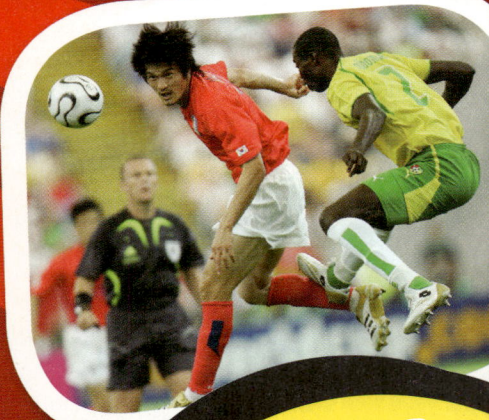

Never to be forgotten moment...
France's midfield superstar **Zinedine Zidane** was sent off in the final for appearing to head-butt former Everton defender **Marco Materazzi** – his last competitive match before hanging up his boots.

35

Countdown to 2010

INTO

THE AFRICAN nations have proved a growing force in world football during recent years. And 2010 gives them a chance to turn up the power even more as the World Cup finals arrive in South Africa. Here's what the competing teams can expect to find...

THE GROUNDS

World Cup games will be played at ten stadiums between June 11 and July 11. If initial ticket applications are anything to go by the grounds will be packed to capacity – more than 500,000 requests to watch games were made within the first month of ticket lines opening.

Soccer City

WHERE: Johannesburg
CAPACITY: 94,700   **BUILT:** 1987

The first international football stadium built in South Africa, this was used for the 1996 Africa Cup of Nations and will host the 2010 World Cup Final.

World Cup officials will be in offices nearby. The stadium, which is designed to look like an African pot, has had its capacity increased by around 15,000.

AFRICA

Ellis Park

WHERE: Johannesburg **CAPACITY:** 70,000 **BUILT:** 1982

Originally built just over 80 years ago as a rugby ground this was demolished and rebuilt and then used for the 1995 Rugby World Cup. It is the home ground of Orlando Pirates FC. Among former players is ex-Bolton and Charlton defender Mark Fish. It has been improved for the finals.

Quick facts

Don't expect to hot-foot it between games or even be able to jump on a bike or bus. Some of the stadiums are **THOUSANDS OF MILES APART** – and involve plane journeys of up to four hours!

53 AFRICAN TEAMS were chasing **FIVE** qualifying places in the finals.

South Africans will be given **FREE TV ACCESS** to all games – and giant screens are expected to be put up in the nine host cities for thousands of other fans to see matches.

South Africa's national side is known as the **BAFANA BAFANA**.

Premier League striker **BENNI MCCARTHY** and midfielder **AARON MOKOENA** are South African internationals, along with Everton's **STEVEN PIENAAR**, Rangers' **DEAN FURMAN** and Norwich midfielder **MATT PATTISON**.

The mascot

ZAKUMI, a leopard, is the official mascot. He is meant to symbolise Africa with his self-confidence, pride, hospitality, social skills and warm-heartedness.

He loves to play football as it is a great way to connect with others and break down language barriers. He always carries his football around and will invite people to play with him.

His name is a composition of 'ZA' standing for South Africa and 'kumi', which translates into 'ten' in various languages across Africa.

Former Leeds United and South Africa skipper Lucas Radebe, said: "He is extremely proud to be the official mascot and determined to be the best host possible for all fans visiting our beloved country of South Africa."

Royal Bafokeng

WHERE: Rustenburg **CAPACITY:** 42,000 **BUILT:** 1999

Named after the Bafokeng people who live in the area, the Palace has staged Premier Soccer League games and World Cup qualifier

Loftus Versfeld

WHERE: Pretoria **CAPACITY:** 45,000 **BUILT:** 1906

A venue for the 2009 FIFA Confederations Cup, the ground was also host to the 1995 Rugby World Cup and 1996 Afric Cup of Nations. Now home to Mamelodi Sundowns.

Peter Mokoba
WHERE: Polokwane **CAPACITY:** 45,000 **BUILT:** 1976

This newly improved ground in the Peter Mokaba Sports Complex is in an area of South Africa with the largest number of registered football players and just a few miles from the city centre.

Nelson Mandella Bay
WHERE: Port Elizabeth **CAPACITY:** 49,500 **BUILT:** 2009

A passionate football area despite not having a top-flight side. Big football games have been played at a local rugby ground. An impressive three tiers high and right next to a lake.

Mbombela Stadium
WHERE: Nelspruit **CAPACITY:** 46,000 **BUILT:** 2009

Mbombela takes its name from the local area. The stadium is a rounded rectangular shape so all seats have a good view. It's about four miles from the city centre.

African Renaissance
WHERE: Cape Town **CAPACITY:** 70,000 **BUILT:** 2009

In the city suburb of Green Point, and close to the sea, the stadium is built on a former golf course. It has been purpose-built for football and is due to host the opening game and a semi-final.

King Senzangakhona
WHERE: Durban **CAPACITY:** 70,000 **BUILT:** 2007

This replaces the city's King's Park and won't look too different to Wembley with two large archways 100 metres above the stadium roof. The ground will later cater for athletics, rugby, golf and swimming.

Final numbers...

5 years just putting together accommodation lists for visiting fans.

47 million people live in South Africa and English is the main language.

74 South Africa caps – a record – won by Shaun Bartlett, the former Charlton striker.

Reflections on the World Cup

Stars of previous finals reveal some of their memories

MICHAEL OWEN

on making his World Cup finals debut at 18

"**GREAT MEMORIES** to have played in the World Cup and to have experienced all that goes with it, especially as I was so young. It was brilliant, although it was a bit of a downer to get knocked out in the second phase. Getting to the World Cup means you have got the chance to perform on the world's biggest stage and against the world's best players. If you have got any ambitions about being a top player you have got to want to play in big competitions like this."

TERRY BUTCHER
a star under Sir Bobby Robson at Italia 90

THE KEY FOR US was that it was a very adaptable squad with a lot of leaders. I wouldn't say I was a leader, but I was one of the experienced ones – Peter Shilton, Mark Wright, Des Walker to a certain degree, Stuart Pearce, Bryan Robson, although he didn't appear in the latter stages. Plus we had people like Chrissie Waddle, Peter Beardsley, Gary Lineker, they are all winners, all strong characters. That was a big, big reason why we went a long way and the team also gelled very well. Whether it was a 4-4-2 or a 3-5-2 it gelled."

CHRIS WADDLE
on that infamous penalty miss

A LOT OF PEOPLE still come up and say 'I'd never have taken one' and I say 'I wish I hadn't'. There were two ways to react; basically you can do a Lord Lucan and disappear or stick your chest out and prove to everybody you're a good footballer. That's the one I opted for. I think the fact I returned to Marseilles rather than England probably helped me get over it. I don't dwell on the memory."

41

DAVID BECKHAM
on his penalty against Argentina in 2002

"**FOR ME, IT WAS** the best and biggest thing that I could've ever done in my career at that time. The moment the ball struck the back of the net, funnily enough, my mind went clear, everything I was thinking, everything I had gone through. I knew how much it meant for me to score that goal for my family, and of course for the fans, because the rivalry against Argentina is huge."

NORMAN WHITESIDE
former Man United star who set a new record at the 1982 finals in Spain…

"**AT 17 I WAS THE YOUNGEST** person to play in the World Cup and at the time there was a lot of attention surrounding me. I was the youngest since Pele, and because we did well [the Irish got through to the second group stage, beating the hosts along the way] it just grew and grew. It's a few years ago now but I don't mind talking about being the 'youngest this or that' at all. It's not a bad thing to be remembered for, is it?"

GARY LINEKER

England's all-time second-best goalscorer.

> **THE HIGHLIGHT** of my two World Cups has to be against Poland in 1986 and scoring the hat-trick. The Poland game transformed things on a personal note, I went on to score a few more goals and win the Golden Boot which earned me a move to Barcelona. The World Cup is special. It's the highest stage that any player can ever perform on. It puts you in the spotlight, but it's also the best chance to test yourself against the best players in the world."

SHAY GIVEN

The Republic of Ireland's most-capped keeper who is aiming to be all-time best

> **PLAYING IN THE 2002** World Cup finals provided my greatest memories in an Ireland shirt and I want more. I often think of the penalty shoot-out against Spain in 2002 and the chances we had during the game."

43

RECORD-

David Beckham and Michael Owen are both chasing very special records at the 2010 World Cup finals

David Beckham

Finals: 1998, 2002, 2006
Games played: 13
Goals: 3 **Yellow cards:** 0
Red cards: 1

IF BOTH PLAYERS appear at the tournament it will be four consecutive finals for the two stars.

Becks has already set a new best for England caps and his recent form at AC Milan means he is likely to be going to South Africa.

Although Owen was off the radar at the start of Fabio Capello's reign as England boss, a return to fitness and goal-scoring form would also see England's second-highest scorer of all-time back in the Three Lions fold.

Other teams and players are also after new bests...

FACT!

David Beckham reached 108 caps in February 2009 when he came on as a sub in the friendly against Spain. That meant he equalled Bobby Moore's record of appearances for an England outfield player.

FACT!

Keeper Peter Shilton has appeared the most times for England but there's a chance Becks can beat his total of 125 caps. If Becks plays a part in every England qualifier and friendly match to the quarter-finals of the World Cup he will beat Shilton's 20-year-old record.

HUNTERS

Michael Owen

Finals: 1998, 2002, 2006
Games played: 12
Goals: 4 **Yellow cards:** 0
Red cards: 0

FACT! Reigning World Champions **Italy** have won the trophy four times and been runners-up twice.

FACT! If **David James** plays in the 2010 World Cup Final he will be just 20 days away from his 40th birthday. Legendary Italy keeper Dino Zoff was 40 when he appeared in the winning side at the 1982 finals.

FACT! **Brazil** have played in every World Cup finals so far and have won the trophy FIVE times. Their legendary player Pele is the only man to have THREE winner's medals.

45

All of the winners